Government Leaders

Then and Now

Lisa Zamosky

Associate Editor
Christina Hill, M.A.

Assistant Editor
Torrey Maloof

Editorial Director
Emily R. Smith, M.A.Ed.

Project Researcher
Gillian Eve Makepeace

Editorial Manager
Gisela Lee, M.A.

Editor-in-Chief
Sharon Coan, M.S.Ed.

Creative Director
Lee Aucoin

Illustration Manager
Timothy J. Bradley

Designers
Lesley Palmer
Debora Brown
Zac Calbert
Robin Erickson

Project Consultant
Corinne Burton, M.A.Ed.

Publisher
Rachelle Cracchiolo, M.S.Ed.

Teacher Created Materials Publishing

5301 Oceanus Drive
Huntington Beach, CA 92649
http://www.tcmpub.com
ISBN 978-0-7439-9386-9

Table of Contents

Government

People who make laws and solve problems form a **government** (GUHV-uhrn-muhnt). There are government leaders all over the world. They may work to help a whole country (KUHN-tree). Or, they may work with a state or a city. These leaders help run our **communities** (kuh-MEW-nuh-tees).

✦ Washington, D.C. is the center of our government.

In this country, we choose our leaders by voting. Any **citizen** (SIT-uh-zuhn) at least 18 years old can vote. We are lucky. Some people in the world do not have that choice.

← This couple is voting in the early 1900s.

The President

Washington, D.C., is a city in the United States. It is also the **capital**. A lot of important leaders live and work there.

The **president** (PREZ-uh-duhnt) is our most important leader. He leads the whole country. He lives in the White House. The president works hard to keep things fair for everyone. And, he makes sure that the laws of the country are followed. Citizens of the United States vote for a new president every four years.

⬇ The president of the United States lives in the White House.

Naming the City

Washington, D.C. was named after George Washington. He was the first president of the United States.

Bright Idea

A man named Alexander Hamilton had a great idea. He wanted to build a capital city. This would be where all the leaders could work. His idea became Washington, D.C.

▲ Alexander Hamilton

Congress

Congress is a part of the government. The people in Congress make laws for the country. And, they work closely with the president.

The **Senate** is one part of Congress. It has 100 members. That is two from every state. The vice president of the United States is the president of the Senate. He votes on laws if there is a tie.

⬆ This is the room where the Senate meets.

Two Days!

Rebecca Felton was the first woman to be a United States senator. But, she was only in office for two days! Then, a new senator took over.

The **House of Representatives** (rep-ri-ZENT-uh-tivz) is the other part of Congress. It is much bigger. It has 435 members. The number of members from each state is different. States with more people have more members.

Congress works in the ➤ Capitol building.

◄ The House of Representatives meets in this room.

Big State

California (kal-uh-FORN-nyuh) has the most members in the House of Representatives. The reason for this is that more people live there than in any other state.

◄ Judges sit in the front of courtrooms.

Judges

Judges (JUHJ-uhz) have important jobs. Judges have to decide what the laws mean. They have to understand the **Constitution** (kon-stih-TOO-shun) of the United States. The laws have to follow what the Constitution says.

Sometimes people cannot agree on things. So, they go to court. A judge decides their cases. The people have to do what the judge says.

Judges can be found at every level of government. They work for cities, states, and the country. The highest court is called the Supreme Court.

First on the Bench

Thurgood Marshall was the first African American to serve on the Supreme Court.

This is the Supreme Court building.

Female Justice

Sandra Day O'Connor was the first woman on the Supreme Court. She served for 24 years.

The governor of Texas ➡ lives in this house.

Governors

The **governor** (GUV-uhr-nuhr) is the leader of a state. Governors make sure that the laws of their states are followed. To do this, they work with other members of state government. Every state has a state Congress. The state congresses help the governors make big decisions (dih-SIZ-uhnz).

State governments have certain jobs they must do. They work to help their citizens. States collect taxes and build roads. They work with local businesses (BIZ-nuhs-uhz). Governors help make plans for their states.

A governor is like a president. Only, he or she is in charge of a state and not a country. Governors learn how to be good leaders. Some governors have gone on to become presidents of the United States.

What's in a Name?

In Germany, the head of the country is called a chancellor (CHAN-suh-ler). But, the leader of Puerto Rico (PWER-toh REE-koh) is called a governor. And, the leader of Great Britain is called a prime minister.

⬆ These men were leaders of Russia and Germany.

Movie Star or Governor?

California is known for its movie stars. But a movie star as a governor? There already have been two! Ronald Reagan (RAY-gahn) and Arnold Schwarzenegger (SCHWARZ-uhn-egg-ur) were once movie stars. Mr. Reagan even went on to become president of the United States.

President Ronald Reagan ➡

↟ President George W. Bush meets with
the governor and mayor of New York.

Mayors

The **mayor** (MAY-uhr) is the leader of a city or
town. For some cities, this is a very big job. New York
City has over 8 million (MIL-yuhn) people. But, there
are some small towns with only a few hundred people.
It is the mayor's job to take care
of these citizens.

Mayors work with other leaders. It is their job
to help the city run well. They have to deal with how
the city spends money. This is called the **budget** (BUD-
juht).

Mayors work on long-term plans. That way, the city will be taken care of for years. They also have to solve daily problems. This might include getting the trash picked up on time.

Tragedy

Rudy Giuliani (JOO-lee-ah-nee) was the mayor of New York City. In September 2001, New York was attacked by terrorists. Mr. Giuliani helped the city get back on its feet.

High School Mayor

In 2005, Michael Sessions was elected as the new mayor of Hillsdale, Michigan. He was only a senior in high school at the time. He won the election by only two votes!

⬆ Michael Sessions is sworn in as mayor.

City or Town Council

There are also city or town **councils** (KOWN-sills). A council is a group of people. They make laws for their community. They work closely with the mayor. Together, they help make their cities and towns great places to live.

These councils have meetings. There, they discuss problems. Citizens can come to these meetings. The council will listen to the concerns of the people. That way, they can solve problems that people might have.

▼ A meeting in Virginia in 1619

A city council meeting in 1959

↑ A Los Angeles school council meeting

School Leaders

Most school districts have a school board. These people meet with citizens and school leaders. They set up all the rules for your school. They can even tell your principal what to do!

HOAs

Some communities have home-owner associations (uh-soh-see-AY-shuhns). They are called HOAs. This is a group of people who live in one neighborhood (NAY-ber-hood). HOAs make rules for neighborhoods.

This is a ballot from 1960.

▲ This man checks voter registrations.

Voting

We vote for most of our government leaders. This means that they are **elected** to office. The voters decide who will win the election. That is why it is so important for people to vote. They vote for the person who they think will do the best job.

People used to vote by filling out pieces of paper. They would drop the papers into a box. Now, there are more ways to vote. You can vote by mail. Or, some places even have voting machines that are computers.

◄ Women in India waiting to vote

The Big Vote

The largest elections of any country were in India. This was in 1984. People voted to fill 542 jobs!

Long Terms

In Italy, citizens vote for a new president every seven years.

▲ This child helps his father vote in Italy.

Choosing Leaders

There are some government leaders who are not elected. Instead, they are **appointed**. This means that they are chosen to do jobs. Mayors and governors appoint people to jobs.

The president appoints people, too. He appoints judges to work for the Supreme Court. The president also chooses his **cabinet**. The cabinet is a group of people who help run the country. The president chooses people who he thinks will best fit each job. But, Congress has to agree with his choices.

◄ President Abraham Lincoln meets with his cabinet members.

Cabinet Members

There are 15 people in the president's cabinet. These men and women are in charge of many parts of the government. They run parks and schools. They work with other countries. They help defend the country against attacks. And, they keep us healthy and safe.

Secretary of
STATE

Secretary of
AGRICULTURE

Secretary of
COMMERCE

Secretary of
DEFENSE

Secretary of
EDUCATION

Secretary of
ENERGY

Secretary of
HEALTH and HUMAN SERVICES

Secretary of
HOMELAND SECURITY

Secretary of
INTERIOR

Secretary of
HOUSING and URBAN DEVELOPMENT

Secretary of
LABOR

Secretary of
TRANSPORTATION

Secretary of
TREASURY

Secretary of
VETERANS AFFAIRS

ATTORNEY GENERAL

⬆ Each of these jobs is a part of the president's cabinet.

Making a Difference

There are many kinds of jobs with the government. These leaders try to make our lives better. They help solve problems. They try to keep our country safe and fair. They do this by passing laws that will help us. Then, they make sure the laws are followed.

▲ A group of children march in a Fourth of July parade.

▲ These people cheer after their governor gives a speech.

Being a government leader is a hard job. These leaders have to be good role models. And, they have to make good decisions. Government leaders help make our country and communities great places to live.

A Day in the Life Then

Jeannette Rankin (1880–1973)

Jeannette Rankin (juh-NET RANK-in) had many jobs throughout her life. She was a teacher and a social worker. She also fought for peace and for women's rights. But, her most important job was as a government leader. She decided to run for Congress. Many people voted for her. She became the first woman elected to the House of Representatives.

Let's pretend to ask Jeanette Rankin some questions about her job.

Why did you decide to run for Congress?

I wanted to make a difference in our country. I think women need to be active in government. Half of the people in this country are women. So, shouldn't half of the members of government be women? I think so!

What is your day like?

My day is very busy. I go to many meetings. I spend a lot of time on the floor of the House. That is where we all meet together as one big group.

What do you like most about your job?

Being a congresswoman is a big job. I try to make sure our country makes good choices. I like that I get to be a part of important decisions. I hope that more women will become government leaders. We need them to represent the women in our country.

This is the room where the House of Representatives meets.

Tools of the Trade Then

This is the Constitution of the United States. It tells how to run the government. The leaders have to follow these rules.

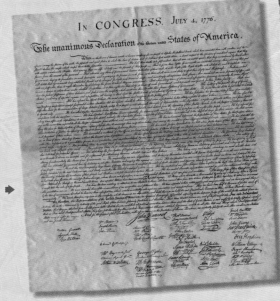

This is the Declaration of Independence. It was written in 1776. This tool allowed America to become its own country.

These women voted in an election long ago. They wrote their votes on slips of paper. Then, they put the papers into a voting box. Someone counted the votes by hand.

Tools of the Trade Now

◆ The telephone is a tool used by many local government leaders. They call people's homes. And, they tell people about their goals as leaders. This can help them win votes.

This is a voting ballot. Today, people ➤ vote in different ways. Some people vote from home. Others use a computer. In some small towns people still use paper ballots.

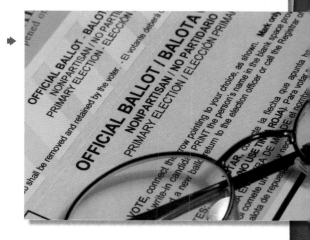

◆ These people are waiting to hear a speech. Speeches have always been important tools. This is how people hear what a government leader plans to do. Today, speeches are on the radio and television. That way, many people can hear them.

A Day in the Life Now

Tony Kawashima

Tony Kawashima (COW-uh-she-muh) is a council member for a city called Tustin. He has done lots of things in city government. He has even been the mayor! Council Member Kawashima is an active member of his community. He does a lot of volunteer work. He is married and has two teenage sons.

Why did you decide to run for city council?

We should all give back to our community. There are many places where you can help. It can be at your school, church, or service club. My wife and I have always helped with our two boys' school activities. Then, the chance came to run for a city council seat. It was exciting to be able to make a difference for a whole city.

What is your day like?

I meet with people and businesses that have concerns. They come to me for advice and help. I attend city council meetings twice a month. I need to read a lot of reports to get ready for the meetings. This is my homework. It helps me to be prepared. That way, I can make good decisions. I also get to attend special events. Often, I get to speak to students at schools.

What do you like most about your job?

I like to help other people. I am happy to know that I've helped someone out. I also enjoy going to schools and speaking about the city of Tustin.

⬥ Kawashima in front of the large airplane hanger in Tustin.

Glossary

appointed—selected to do a job

budget—a plan for using money

cabinet—people who work to help the president lead the country

capital—city where the government is run

citizen—person living in a city or town who has the right to vote

communities—groups of people living in the same areas

Congress—the part of the United States government that makes laws for the country

Constitution—the laws of the United States

councils—the leading group in cities or towns

elected—selected by vote for a job

government—the people and offices that rule over a country, state, or city

governor—leader of a state

House of Representatives—a part of the United States Congress; based on population

judges—public officers who hear and decide court cases

mayor—leader of a city or town

president—the leader of the country

Senate—a part of the United States Congress; two senators per state

Index

Credits

Acknowledgements

Special thanks to Tony Kawashima and the city of Tustin for providing the *Day in the Life Now* interview. Mr. Kawashima is a council member in Tustin, California.

Image Credits

front cover Luke Frazza/AFP/Getty Images; p.1 Luke Frazza/AFP/Getty Images; p.4 The Library of Congress; p.5 The Library of Congress; p.6 Photos.com; p.7 (top) The Library of Congress; p.7 (top) Hemera Technologies, Inc.; p.7 (bottom) The Library of Congress; p.8 (top) U.S. Senate Historical Office; p.8 (bottom) The Library of Congress; p.9 (top) Photos.com; p.9 (middle) U.S. Senate Historical Office; p.9 (bottom left) Cartesia; p.9 (bottom right) Hemera Technologies, Inc; p.10 iStockphoto.com/Frances Twitty; p.11 (top) The Library of Congress; p.11 (bottom) Photos.com; p.12 Jim Steinhart/travelphotobase.com; p.13 (top) Marcus Brandt/AFP/Getty Images; p.13 (bottom) The National Archives; p.14 Paul J. Richards/AFP/Getty Images; p.15 (top) Jed Jacobsohn/Getty Images; p.15 (bottom) Bill Pugliano/Getty Images; p.16 The Granger Collection, New York; p.17 (top) Ed Clark/Time Life Pictures/Getty Images; p.17 (bottom) J. Emilio Flores/Getty Images; p.18 (left) Lisa McDonald/BigStockPhoto; p.18 (right) The National Archives; p.19 (top) STR/AFP/Getty Images; p.19 (bottom) Andreas Solaro/AFP/Getty Images; p.20 The Granger Collection, New York; p.21 Teacher Created Materials; p.22 iStockphoto.com/Stefan Klein; p.23 HumbyValdes/Shutterstock, Inc.; p.24 The Library of Congress; p.25 The Library of Congress; p.26 (top) The National Archives; p.26 (middle) Historical Documents Co.; p.26 (bottom) The Library of Congress; p.27 (top) János Gehring/Shutterstock, Inc.; p.27 (middle) Stephen Coburn/Shutterstock, Inc.; p.27 (bottom) Ryan Photo Studio/Shutterstock, Inc.; p.28 Courtesy of Tony Kawashima; p.29 Courtesy of Tony Kawashima; back cover The Library of Congress